THE BUMPER BOOK OF KERRYMAN JOKES

The Bumper Book of
Kerryman Jokes

DES MacHALE

THE MERCIER PRESS

The Mercier Press Limited
4 Bridge Street, Cork
24 Lower Abbey Street, Dublin 1

ISBN 0 85342 666 X

Cartoons by B. O'Brien and M. Dubrett

Reprinted 1984, 1987, 1990.

I dedicate this book
to my daughter Catherine
But what do I do if
She marries a Kerryman?

Printed in Ireland by Litho Press Co., Midleton, Co. Cork.

Introduction

Have you heard about the Kerryman who bought two copies of *THE BUMPER BOOK OF KERRYMAN JOKES* to mend his damaged car? Seriously folks, this bumper book is the biggest and best collection of Kerryman jokes ever published. Reports of the death of this art form have been greatly exaggerated and I find it little short of amazing that good new Kerryman jokes seem to surface all the time.

Those who enjoyed my three previous books, *The Book of Kerryman Jokes, The Worst Kerryman Jokes,* and *The Official Kerryman Jokebook,* often ask me where Kerryman jokes come from. Well, I've manufactured a fair share of them myself, but my own belief is that the vast majority are concocted by Kerrymen themselves to make the rest of us feel a bit better about the fact that we are not sons of the Kingdom. Kerrymen *know* they are superior and no other Irish county could have absorbed in such a good humoured way so many jokes directed against themselves over the last ten years and come back smiling looking for more.

The following is a true story. A friend of mine told me that while he enjoyed my books he found them very expensive. I told him he was getting good value — three good guaranteed Irish jokes for a penny but then he told me how much he had paid for one book, mentioning a figure over three times the retail price. 'Where did you pay that for it?' I asked in disbelief. 'Tralee,' he replied sheepishly!

A businessman hired a Kerry girl as his private secretary but after a week noticed that she was no longer answering the phone. When asked for an explanation she said, 'What's the point? Nine times out of ten it's for you any-way.'

Have you heard about the Kerry clairvoyant?
He could look into the past.

What does a Kerryman take with him to a cock fight?
His duck.

How do you know if a Kerry cock fight is rigged?
The duck wins.

A tourist passing through Kerry saw a loaf of bread sitting in the middle of the road, so he took it to the local Garda Station.
He was told to hold on to it for thirty days and if nobody claimed it he could keep it.

Kerry undertakers have just gone on an all-out strike. However, they are going to provide a skeleton service to handle emergencies.

Two Kerrymen made the Irish bobsleigh team for the Winter Olympics. However, they refused to take part in the heats until the track was gritted.

Where would you find a Kerryman the day his boat comes in?
Waiting at the airport.

Have you heard about the Kerryman who used to take two hot water bottles to bed with him?
It was just in case one of them sprang a leak.

A Kerryman went up to Dublin on a day trip and was stopped by an American tourist who asked him what time it was.
'I'm sorry,' said the Kerryman, 'I'm a stranger here myself.'

A Kerryman has just been made Minister for Defence.
His first task is to have de fence painted.

A Kerryman was out for a ride on his donkey when the animal took fright, bolted and finally wound up with one of his hind legs caught in one of the stirrups.
'Hold on a minute,' said the Kerryman. 'If you're getting on then I'm getting off.'

Sticker seen on a Kerryman's car —
THANK YOU FOR NOT LAUGHING AT THIS CAR.

What organisation has the following uniform:—
A purple three-cornered hat with a green feather, scarlet tunic, canary yellow trousers, and white sequined boots?
The Kerry secret service.

A Kerryman walked into a post office and asked the girl behind the counter, 'What's the postage on a letter bomb?'

Have you heard about the Kerry Boat People?
They've just been sighted off the coast of Vietnam and the Vietnamese Government are going to take fifty of them in.

A Kerryman applying for a job was asked by his prospective employer how many honours in his Leaving Certificate he had.
'Fifty-three,' said the Kerryman.
'You must be joking,' said the employer.
'Well you started it,' said the Kerryman.

Two Kerrymen had been marooned on a desert island for several weeks and were running out of food and water.
'We've had it,' said the first, 'nothing can rescue us now.'
'Hold on,' said the second, 'we're saved, here comes the Titanic.'

A Kerryman was asked in a survey what he thought of the United Nations.
'It was fine', he replied, 'until they started letting all those foreigners into it'.

A KERRYMAN'S DIGITAL COMPUTER—WITH MEMORY

ALSO AVAILABLE IN LEFT HAND MODEL

Have you heard about the Kerry video recorder?
It records the programmes you don't want to see and shows them when you're out of the house.

A Kerryman went to Liverpool and was having a drink with his friends.
'Try to be sophisticated,' his friends told him, 'and when the barman asks you what you are having, say you'll have a lager and lime.'
'Right,' said the Kerryman, and proceeded to place his order.
'How much lime sir?' asked the barman.
'About a shovelful,' said the Kerryman.

'A rainbow,' a Kerryman once declared, 'is not really an optical illusion, it only looks like one'.

Have you heard about the new waterproof watch invented by a Kerryman?
It comes filled with water and you can't get it out no matter how hard you try.

Want to get your name in print? Just send £50 to the new Kerry Directory of Confidence Trick Victims.

Have you heard about the Kerry businessman who returned his dictaphone and complained that it spoke with a Kerry accent?

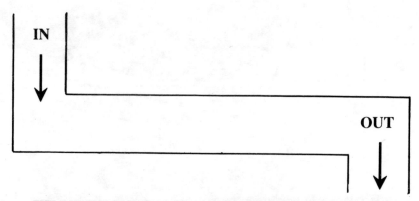

**THE FAMOUS KERRY MAZE — A RESCUE SERVICE IS AVAILABLE
FOR THOSE WHO GET LOST INSIDE.
SOME KERRYMEN HAVE DIFFICULTY FINDING THEIR WAY IN.**

SOME KERRY JURY VERDICTS

WE FIND THE MAN WHO STOLE THE MARE NOT GUILTY.

WE RETURN A VERDICT OF GUILTY AGAINST THE UNKNOWN MURDERER WHO KILLED O'SULLIVAN.

NOT GUILTY, BUT WE RECOMMEND HE DOESN'T DO IT AGAIN.

UNANIMOUS — NINE TO THREE.

YOUR HONOUR, WE ARE ALL OF ONE MIND — INSANE.

NOT GUILTY — IF HE'LL PROMISE TO EMIGRATE.

WE FIND THE PRISONER GUILTY AND RECOMMEND THAT HE BE HANGED, AND WE HOPE IT WILL BE A WARNING TO HIM.

JUDGE TO DEFENDANT: YOU MAY LEAVE THE COURTROOM A FREE MAN WITH NO STAIN ON YOUR CHARACTER EXCEPT FOR THE FACT THAT YOU WERE ACQUITTED BY A KERRY JURY.

WE THE JURY WOULD HAVE GIVEN ANYTHING TO HAVE SEEN THE FIGHT.

IN A KERRY GROCERY STORE

> **MOTHERS ARE REQUESTED NOT TO LEAVE THEIR BABIES SITTING ON THE BACON SLICER BECAUSE WE ARE GETTING A LITTLE BEHIND WITH OUR ORDERS**

SOME FAMOUS KERRYMEN

SEÁN D'OLIER — Famous for hanging from the ceiling.

RICK O'SHEA — Famous for banging his head off the wall.

EOGHAN CASH — The famous Kerry bankrupt.

NICK McGUINNESS — Famous for stealing other people's pints.

MICK DAWIRE — The famous Kerry electrician.

SEÁN Ó SÚILAMHÁIN — The famous one-eyed Kerryman.

PAT PENDING — The famous inventor from Kerry.

DON DIGGIN — The famous retired Kerry undertaker.

PHIL McCAVITY — The famous Kerry dentist.

EVEL O'KNEIVEL — He jumped over twenty motorbikes in a double-decker bus.

P. KING AND HIS WIFE NAN KING — The famous Chinese Kerry couple.

COWJACK — The famous Kerry detective.

THE JAP OF DUNLOE — The famous yellow skinned Kerryman.

NELLY SAVALAS — The famous bald Kerrywoman.

AMAN DINGLE AND KUNTA KIAREE — Stars of the blockbuster T.V. series **Boots**.

NICK O'TEEN — Introduced tobacco into Kerry.

SOME KERRY INVENTIONS

THE ONE-PIECE JIGSAW PUZZLE

THE INFLATABLE DARTBOARD for campers

EJECTOR SEATS for /helicopters

AN INDEX TO THE DICTIONARY

CONTACT LENSES WITH FRAMES

PEEP-TOED GALOSHES

A FLOODLIT SUNDIAL FOR NIGHT USE

THE SILENT ALARM CLOCK (WHICH WON THE NOBELL PRIZE)

A PARACHUTE THAT OPENS ON IMPACT

A UNISEX MATERNITY HOSPITAL

A CURE FOR WHICH THERE WAS NO KNOWN DISEASE

A PLAN TO STRAIGHTEN THE LEANING TOWER OF PISA

BOIL-IN-THE-BAG CORNFLAKES

A BAR OF SOAP WITH A HOLE IN THE CENTRE TO AVOID HAVING AWKWARD LITTLE PIECES LEFT AT THE END

COW PÂTÉ

IN A KERRY BEAUTY PARLOUR

```
EARS PIERCED
WHILE YOU WAIT
```

Two Kerryman were walking down the street when one turned to the other and said, 'Look, there's a dead pigeon.'
'Where? Where?' said the second Kerryman, looking up at the sky.

The Parish Priest in a little Kerry church was astonished to see a Kerryman doing the Stations of the Cross starting at the fourteenth and working backwards.
'That's not the way to do it,' said the Parish Priest, 'you've got to start at number one.'
'I thought there was something wrong all right,' said the Kerryman, 'He seemed to be getting better.'

At a Kerry court case the judge said: 'Will the defendant please rise,' and one of the jurymen stood up.
'How come,' asked the judge, 'that you the defendant are on the jury?'
'I don't know,' said the Kerryman sheepishly, 'I thought I was kinda lucky.'

Have you heard about the new game that's all the rage?
It's called Kerry Roulette — you simply bang your head against the wall six times, once very hard.

A Kerryman walked into a bar and said to the barman, 'Give me a Martinus.'
'Surely you mean a Martini, sir,' said the barman.
'Look,' said the Kerryman, 'if I want two, I'll ask for them.'

What happens when you peel a Kerry onion?
It makes you laugh.

Have you heard about the Kerryman who died as a result of too much drink?
He was run over by a Guinness lorry.

A Kerryman went up to Dublin for the All-Ireland Final and had a drop too much to drink on the Saturday night before the match. At about eleven o'clock he hailed a taxi and said to the driver, 'Drive me round St Stephen's Green four hundred times, and step on it, I'm in a hurry.'

HAVE YOU HEARD ABOUT THE KERRYMAN

Who used to wear a wig with a big hole in the middle?
He figured that if he looked bald people wouldn't realise he was wearing a wig.

Who saw a notice 'Please Mind the Step' in a shop?
He had to wait over an hour until someone else came along to mind it for him.

Who ate fifty packets of cornflakes?
He died of sunstroke.

Whose library was burned down?
Both books were destroyed and one of them hadn't even been coloured in.

Who went to a drive-in movie?
He didn't like the show so he slashed the seats.

Who won the Nobel Prize for agriculture?
He was simply a man outstanding in his own field.

Who tried to blow up a bus?
He burned his lips on the exhaust pipe.

Who drove his car into a lake?
He wanted to dip the headlights.

Who drove his car over a cliff?
He wanted to test the air brakes.

SIGN IN A KERRY TOILET

> # PLEASE DO NOT EAT THE LARGE POLO MINTS IN THE URINALS

Two Kerrymen were sitting in a pub.
'Could you tell me the time?' asked the first.
'Certainly I could,' said the second.
'Thank you very much,' said the second Kerryman.

Have you heard about the Kerry operatic tenor who was given seventeen encores at La Scala, Milan?
The audience wouldn't let him leave the stage until he sang the piece properly.

A company selling hair restorer once received the following testimonial from a Kerryman:—

Dear Sir,
    Before using your hair restorer I had three bald patches. Now I have only one.

Have you heard about the Kerryman who went to England and made big money there but wound up in jail?
The money was just a quarter of an inch too big.

Kerry businessman: 'Where's my pencil?'
Secretary: 'It's behind your ear sir.'
Kerry businessman: 'Look, I'm a busy man, which ear?'

A Kerryman was speaking in a debate about the evils of slaughtering animals.
'How about those people who kill pigs,' he thundered, 'despite the fact that they give us such lovely bacon'.

A ninety-two year old Kerryman and his ninety year old wife have just applied for a divorce. They were waiting for their children to die.

Have you heard about the Kerry salesman who only got two orders in an entire week?
They were 'get out' and 'stay out'.

A Kerryman wrote a postcard to his girlfriend and wrote above her address PRIVATE AND CONFIDENTIAL.

EXAMINATION TO BECOME A KERRYMAN

Instructions to Candidates

(a) Answer only one question at a time.

(b) Do not attempt to write on both sides of the paper at the same time.

(c) Slide Rules O.K.

(d) Candidates found cheating will be given extra marks for initiative.

(e) Extra marks for creative spellings.

(f) No point copying from the student in front of you — he probably knows less than you do.

(g) Time allowed — until the cows come home.

1.   WHO WON THE FIRST WORLD WAR? Who came second?

2.   EXPLAIN IN ONE SENTENCE EINSTEIN'S THEORY OF RELATIVITY *OR* Write your name in block capitals.

3.   Is this a question?

4.   NAME THE ODD MAN OUT: The Pope, The Chief Rabbi, The Yorkshire Ripper, The Archbishop of Canterbury.

5.   What is the number of this question?

6.   AT WHAT TIME IS THE NINE O'CLOCK NEWS BROADCAST?

7.   SPELL EACH OF THE FOLLOWING WORDS: dog, cat, pig.

8.   WRITE A TONGUE TWISTER THREE TIMES QUICKLY.

9.   THERE HAVE BEEN TWO KINGS OF ENGLAND NAMED CHARLES. THE FIRST WAS CHARLES THE FIRST — NAME THE OTHER ONE.

10. MAGELLAN MADE THREE TRIPS AROUND THE WORLD AND DIED ON ONE OF THEM. WHICH ONE?

11. Ignore this question completely.

12. THE KERRYMAN JOKE IS THE HIGHEST FORM OF ART (Shakespeare). Discuss.

13. Didn't he go very sudden in the end?

A Kerryman rang the Post Office and said, 'The cord of my telephone is too long. I nearly tripped on it the other day. Would you mind giving it a pull at your end?'

Have you heard about the Kerry air force recruit who jumped out of a plane at 20,000ft without a parachute because he was only practising?

Two Kerrymen were pilot and co-pilot of a Jumbo jet. One day coming in to Shannon Airport they overshot the runway and had to take the aircraft back up again and circle the airport. It happened a second time but at the third attempt, with a superhuman effort, the plane was brought to a halt only six inches from the grass edge.
'Do you know,' said the first Kerryman, 'that's the shortest runway I've ever come across.'
'Well it's the widest one I've ever come across,' said the second Kerryman.

A Kerryman went to college and got B.A., M.A., and Ph.D. degrees in literature but couldn't get a job, so he went to England to work on the buildings. The foreman decided to give him a test before he would take him on.
'What's the difference between a joist and a girder?' he asked.
'Well,' said the Kerryman, 'Joyce wrote Ulysses and Goethe wrote Faust.'

Two Kerrymen were at a bingo session and one of them kept looking over the other's shoulder and telling him when his numbers were being called.
The second Kerryman got annoyed and said, 'Look, why don't you fill in your own card?'
'I can't,' said the first Kerryman, 'it's full.'

Two Corkmen and a Kerryman were about to be shot by firing squad so they decided to try and divert their executioners and escape in the resulting confusion.
'Air-Raid,' shouted the first Corkman, and made his escape as the guards took cover.
'Avalanche,' shouted the second Corkman and he too got away.
'Fire,' shouted the Kerryman.

HOW ABOUT

THE KERRY FIRE EXTINGUISHER FACTORY?
It was burned to the ground.

THE KERRY TADPOLE?
He turned into a butterfly.

THE KERRY GHOST?
He didn't believe in people.

THE KERRY MOSQUITO?
He caught malaria.

THE KERRY GEMINI MAN?
He presses a button and his watch disappears.

THE KERRY MAFIA?
They threaten not to beat people up if they don't pay them money.

THE KERRY NURSE?
She used to wake patients up to give them their sleeping tablets.

THE KERRY EXPEDITION TO CLIMB EVEREST?
They ran out of scaffolding thirty feet from the top.

THE KERRY INSTITUTE FOR ADVANCED STUDIES?
It teaches fractions and long division.

THE KERRY DWARF WHO WAS FIVE FEET TALL?
He claimed he was the tallest dwarf in the world.

THE KERRY TURKEY?
He kept looking forward to Christmas.

THE KERRY FATTED CALF?
He said 'O goody here comes the Prodigal Son.'

SOME KERRY EPITAPHS

HERE LIES
THE BODY OF
MICK MURPHY
— HIS WIDOW MARY
LIVES IN KILLARNEY
AND YEARNS
TO BE
COMFORTED

HERE LIES
THE BODY OF
JOHN O'SULLIVAN
WHO WAS LOST AT SEA
AND NEVER RECOVERED.
HAD HE LIVED HE WOULD
HAVE BEEN BURIED HERE.

IN MEMORY OF
JOHN O'DONOGHUE
WHO WAS FATALLY
BURNED BY
AN EXPLOSION OF A LAMP
FILLED WITH MURPHY'S
NON-EXPLOSIVE BURNING
FLUID.

THIS STONE WAS ERECTED
TO THE MEMORY OF
DIN JOE O'CONNELL
WHO WAS DROWNED
IN THE LAKES
OF KILLARNEY
BY A FEW OF HIS
DEAREST FRIENDS

SOME KERRY WILLS

I LEAVE EVERYTHING TO MYSELF

I LEAVE ALL MY MONEY AND POSSESSIONS TO THE DOCTOR WHO WILL PULL ME THROUGH MY FINAL ILLNESS.

THEN THERE WAS THE KERRYMAN WHO DIDN'T MAKE ANY WILL AT ALL BECAUSE HE THOUGHT IT WOULD BE A DEAD GIVEAWAY TO HIS RELATIVES.

HOW ABOUT THE KERRY LAWYER WHO DIED INTESTATE AS THE RESULT OF AN ACCIDENT?

TO MY ELDEST SON I LEAVE THE FARM AND TO MY SECOND SON I LEAVE MY SEAT IN THE DÁIL.

I WISH TO BE BURIED AT SEA — HIS SON WAS DROWNED DIGGING THE GRAVE.

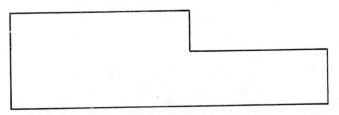

COFFIN FOR A ONE-LEGGED KERRYMAN

A Sign Seen in Kerry

FOR SALE
TOMBSTONE
BARGAIN TO ANYONE NAMED MURPHY

A HINT OF GAELIC

WHAT'S A BIAFRAN?
A Kerryman who goes to Mass twice on Sundays.

WHAT'S AN OSCILLATOR?
A Kerryman who eats donkeys.

IF BLARNEY CASTLE COULD TALK, WHAT WOULD IT SAY?
Póg mo stone.

HAVE YOU HEARD ABOUT THE KERRYMAN WHO HAD A RE-
LAPSE OF MEASLES?
It was a case of Arash Arís.

BUALADH BOS IS A CRASH BETWEEN TWO CIE DOUBLE
DECKERS

What would you call an Indian draper living in Kerry?
MAHATMA GEANSAÍ.

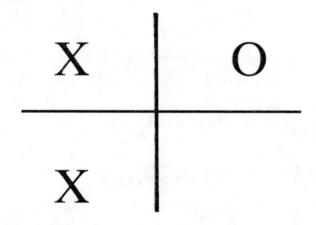

KERRY NAUGHTS AND CROSSES

Why did the Kerryman visit the RTE newsroom?
He wanted to know where they got all the ideas for the news.

Have you heard about the Kerry Isaac Newton?
The apple tree fell on him and broke his neck.

Then there was the Kerryman who lost his job and was replaced by a pocket calculator.

Did you hear about the Kerryman who sold doughnuts to midgets as toilet seats?

Why did the Kerryman stop using egg shampoo?
The hen kept falling off his head.

Have you heard about the Kerry cricket match that was cancelled because both sides showed up wearing the same colours?

A dead Kerryman lay smiling in his coffin.
His wife explained to a friend, 'He's smiling because he died in his sleep and he doesn't know he's dead yet. He's dreaming he's still alive, so when he wakes up and find's he's dead the shock will kill him.'

Have you heard about the latest Kerry invention?
A hairdryer which works under water.

NOTICE IN A KERRY GOLF CLUB

**TROUSERS MAY NOW BE WORN
BY LADIES ON THE COURSE
— BUT THEY MUST BE REMOVED
BEFORE ENTERING THE CLUBHOUSE**

THICKSILVER

What's your name?
STOP THE LIGHTS.

Name two days of the week that begin with the letter 'T'.
TODAY AND TOMORROW.

What was Hitler's first name?
HEIL.

What's the best way to prevent forest fires?
CUT DOWN ALL THE TREES.

Can you tell me the nationality of Napoleon?
COURSE I CAN.
Correct!

How many kinds of pedestrian crossings are there?
Two.
THOSE WHO MAKE IT AND THOSE WHO DON'T.

Who was born in a stable and has millions of followers?
ARKLE.

Why do surgeons wear masks over their faces?
SO THAT IF THE PATIENT DIES NO ONE WILL KNOW WHO DID IT.

What creature eats the least?
THE MOTH — HE JUST EATS HOLES.

Who invented the aspirin?
MOTHER MARY AIKENHEAD.

Who were Adam and Eve's children?
THAT'S A TRICK QUESTION — ADAM AND EVE HAD NO
CHILDREN.

A Kerryman tying his shoelace

METRICATION OFFICE
100 YARDS ⟶

A SIGN SEEN IN KERRY

SOME KERRY GRAFFITI

JOHN LENNON KILLED J.R.

ELVIS IS STILL DEAD.

I'M A KERRYMAN AND PROWD OF IT.

THANK GOD I'M AN ATHEIST.

THERE'S NO POINT VOTING IN ELECTIONS —
THE GOVERNMENT ALWAYS WINS ANYWAY.

SUPPORT THE KERRY LEFT-HANDED CHESS
CHAMPIONSHIPS.

KEEP KERRY TIDY —
DUMP YOUR RUBBISH IN CORK.

ABOLISH HIRE EDUCATION.

HELP STAMP OUT QUICKSAND.

NEVER MAKE A TASK OF PLEASURE AS THE KERRYMAN
SAID AS HE DUG HIS MOTHER-IN-LAW'S GRAVE ONLY
THREE FEET DEEP.

PLEASE RING BELL FOR PORTER
— WHY CAN'T THE PORTER RING THE BELL FOR HIMSELF?

IN A KERRY BARBERS

WE PAY 10p FOR EVERY TIME
THE BARBER'S HAND SLIPS AND HE DRAWS BLOOD —
SOME CUSTOMERS LEAVE HERE WITH A HANDSOME PROFIT

THICKSILVER

What was Ghandi's first name?
GOOSEY GOOSEY.

Name three women prime ministers.
MRS THATCHER, MRS GHANDI AND BEAN UÍ SADAR.

What do the letters AIB stand for?
ARTIFICIAL INSEMINATION BY A BULL.

Why is a giraffe's neck so long?
IT HAS TO BE BECAUSE HIS HEAD IS SO FAR AWAY FROM HIS BODY.

To which family does the whale belong?
I DON'T KNOW. NO FAMILY LIVING NEAR ME HAS ONE ANYWAY.

In anatomy where is the lumbar region?
IS IT IN THE NORTH OF CANADA?

How many degrees in a circle?
HOW BIG A CIRCLE ARE YOU TALKING ABOUT?

What is meant by General Amnesty?
HE WAS THE COMMANDER OF THE ALLIED FORCES DURING THE WAR.

What goes green, amber, red, green, amber, red?
A PACKET OF FRUIT GUMS.

What is backgammon?
IT'S A SORT OF RASHER.

Name two T.V. programmes about potatoes.
CHIPS AND MASH.

Soon after the Department of Agriculture introduced its Premium Bull Scheme, a Kerryman hired the best bull in the country to service his cows. After nearly a month the bull hadn't been returned, so the Department dispatched an inspector hotfoot to Kerry to see what the situation was. He found the bull pulling a plough round a field, the Kerryman whipping him along and shouting, 'Get along outa that, ye bugger ye, that'll teach you there's more to life than romance'.

A consortium of Kerry businessmen have put together twenty million pounds to raise the Titanic.
They've just raised the iceberg.

Have you heard about the Kerryman who got a BA degree in Computer Science and Art?
He got a job painting computers.

One Kerryman met another who was wearing a beautiful £500 mohair suit though it was a bit on the big side for him.
'That's a lovely suit,' said the first Kerryman, 'where did you buy that?'
'Actually,' said the second Kerryman, 'I didn't buy it at all — it was a present from the wife. I came home early from work one day and found it lying on the bed.'

Have you heard about the enthusiastic Kerry Guard who once summoned a motorist for having bald tyres?
The case was dismissed because it turned out the fellow was driving a steam-roller.

What is the definition of an optimist?
A penniless Kerryman ordering oysters in a posh hotel in the hope that he can pay the bill with the pearls.

Kerryman jokes are not new. In 1423 the inhabitants of a little Kerry village built a ten foot wall around the village to keep the Plague out.

Kerry doctor: 'Have you taken this patient's temperature?'
Kerry nurse: 'No. If it's missing, it wasn't me who took it.'

Letter from a Kerryman's mother

Dear Son,

I haven't written to you since the last time I wrote. I'm writing this very slowly because I know you can't read very quickly. If you don't get this letter write and let me know at once. When you write there is no need to put our address on the envelope as the postman knows well enough where we live by now.

We went to Ballybunion for a week this summer and it only rained twice — the first time for three days and the second time for four days. Your father has a great new job where he is over five hundred men — he's cutting the grass in the local cemetery. Your Aunt Mary has just had her appendix taken out and a new washing machine installed. Your Uncle Tom, the one who drank ten glasses of liver salts every day for the last forty years, died last week. We had to beat his liver to death with a stick. The people next door are keeping pigs in their back-yard. We only got wind of it yesterday. Your Uncle Frank who works in the brewery was drowned last week in a big vat of beer. He didn't have a painful death though because he got out three times to go to the gents.

I'm sending you three socks by parcel post as you said in your last letter that you had grown another foot since you left home. I'm also sending you a new jacket and to save weight I have cut off all the buttons. You'll find them in the pocket.

May God protect you
from your loving Mother

P.S. I would have enclosed five pounds but I had already sealed the envelope.

HOW ABOUT

The Kerry Picket?
It went on stike.

The Kerry jellyfish?
It set.

The Kerry Tug-of-War Team?
They were disqualified for pushing.

The Kerry grandmother who went on the pill?
She didn't want any more grandchildren.

The Kerry helicopter pilot who felt a bit cold?
He turned the fan off.

The Kerry explorer who paid £10 for a sheet of sandpaper?
He thought it was a map of the Sahara Desert.

A KERRY CHESS BOARD

The Kerryman who was taking his driving test?
He opened the door to let the clutch out.

The Kerryman who bought a black and white dog?
He figured the licence would be cheaper than for a coloured one.

The Kerry kidnapper?
He enclosed a stamped addressed envelope with the ransom note.

The Kerry soldier?
He went into Fota zoo, shot six gorillas and freed the ostriches.

The eighty-year-old Kerryman who married an eighty-five-year-old wife?
He wanted someone to answer the Rosary for him. They spent the entire honeymoon trying to get out of the car.

The Kerry comedian who quit the stage?
People kept on laughing at him.

The Kerry sailor who claimed the Irish Navy was much better than the British Navy?
When he was in the Irish Navy he could go home for his tea every evening.

The Kerryman who spent an hour in a big store looking for a cap with a peak at the back?

The Kerryman who was stranded for an hour in a supermarket when the escalator broke down?

The Kerry plastic surgeon?
He sat near the fire and melted.

The Kerry schoolboy who used to play truant from school on Saturday?

The Kerry boy who swallowed a fifty-pence piece because it was his lunch money?

SOME KERRY INVENTIONS

A NEW KIND OF BREAD.
So light that a pound of it weighed only four ounces.

THE WORLD'S STRONGEST GLUE
But the inventor couldn't get the top off the bottle.

A NEW PILL GUARANTEED TO CURE LOSS OF MEMORY
But the inventor couldn't remember what it was for.

A MECHANICAL WEATHER FORECASTER
Consisting of a piece of old rope. When the rope moves over and back it's
windy and when the rope gets wet it's raining.

A CURE TO HELP YOU FORGET ALL ABOUT AMNESIA

A WOODEN SUBSTITUTE FOR MARBLE
That was so realistic that it sank as soon as you put it in water.

INFLAMMABLE ASBESTOS
That can be disposed of by burning.

A ROLL-BAR FOR MOTOR BOATS

A FLOODLIT SUNDIAL

BURNED OUT LIGHTBULBS FOR DARKROOMS

A NEW CURE FOR SEASICKNESS
Sit under a tree.

SIGN IN A KERRY AUCTIONEERS

> THE HIGHEST BIDDER TO BE THE PURCHASER
> — UNLESS SOMEBODY BIDS MORE

First Kerry poet: 'How are things with you?'
Second Kerry poet: 'Not too good, I can't get my latest poem finished. I've been looking for a single word for two weeks.'
First Kerry poet: 'How about a fortnight?'

Have you heard about the Kerryman who has stopped putting his clock forward every year?
It kept falling off the mantelpiece.

One Saturday the *Cork Examiner* announced that it was increasing its price by two pence on the following Monday.
A Kerryman went out and bought all the copies he could find on Saturday.

Have you heard about the Kerryman who had a false wisdom tooth fitted?

A Kerryman and his wife went on holiday to London and stayed at the Savoy Hotel. When they returned home the wife remarked to a neighbour, 'What upset Dinny most was that the manager of the hotel had never even heard of him. Sure in Kerry he's world famous.'

A Kerryman went to his psychiatrist and told him he was worried because he had a collection of over ten thousand L.P. records and couldn't stop buying them.
'There's nothing to worry about,' said the psychiatrist, 'I like to play records myself.'
'Oh, I don't play them,' said the Kerryman, 'I just collect the holes in the middle.'

'You are charged,' said the Judge to a Kerryman, 'with having wilfully, feloniously and with malice aforethought appropriated to your own use and behoof a certain article, to wit, a bovine quadruped — the said quadruped having been wrongfully and feloniously abstracted by you from the estate of one Daniel Murphy on or about the fourth day of July, *Anno Domini* 1980, contrary to the law of the land. How do you plead?'
'Not guilty, your honour,' said the Kerryman, 'all I did was steal a cow.'

A KERRY MINE DETECTOR

HOW DO YOU RECOGNISE

A KERRY PIRATE?
He's got a patch over each eye.

A KERRY BRIDE?
She's the one with the white wellies.

A KERRY BATH?
It's got taps at both ends to keep the water level.

A KERRY BUSINESS EXECUTIVE?
He's the one wearing the pin stripe wellies.

A KERRY STRING QUARTET?
They stop every few minutes to clear the saliva from their instruments.

A KERRYMAN'S MATCHED LUGGAGE?
Two plastic bags from the same supermarket.

A KERRY CARD SHARP?
He plays the one card trick.

A KERRY HIPPIE? Flared wellies.

A KERRY AIRCRAFT?
It's got outside toilets.

A TOPLESS KERRY RESTAURANT?
It's got no roof.

A KERRY STREAKER? He's fully clothed.

A KERRY SUBMARINE? It's got half doors.

A Kerryman got out of jail digging a tunnel and climbing over a two hundred foot wall. So he rang the jail and asked if he could speak to himself, prisoner 36129.

The jailer said, 'I'll check sir,' and came back in a few minutes and reported that that particular prisoner's cell seemed to be empty.

'Hurrah,' said the Kerryman, 'I've escaped.'

First Kerryman: 'What's Mick's other name?'
Second Kerryman: 'Mick who?'

A Kerryman was once charged with attacking a Corkman with a razor.
He was acquitted because he hadn't plugged it in.

Have you heard about the Kerryman who used to eat nothing except paper clips?
His doctor had put him on a staple diet.

A Kerryman had a drop too much to drink so he was taken to the Station and asked to walk the white line. He refused to do it without a safety net.

How do you ask a Kerryman for change?
Say, 'Can you give me two tens for a five?'
If he complains say, 'I was only joking, give me back my two tens, here's your five.'

How do you recognise a Kerry Hippy?
He keeps plastic marijuana plants in his greenhouse.

One morning a Kerryman got a parcel in the post marked in large red letters HANDLE WITH CARE. Excitedly he opened it and inside he found a handle.

First Kerry workman: 'Have you that hammer Mick?'
Second Kerry workman: 'I have.'
First Kerry workman: 'Where have you it?'
Second Kerry workman: 'I have it lost.'

HAVE YOU HEARD ABOUT THE KERRYMAN

WHO JOINED THE NAVY?
He was given a job as a deckhand on a submarine.

WHO JOINED THE 'SAVE ENERGY CAMPAIGN'?
He stopped working.

WHO BECAME A DIRECTOR IN A FILM BUSINESS?
He got a job as a cinema usher.

WHO WENT PLAYING WATER POLO?
His horse was drowned.

WHO SET FIRE TO HIS JACKET?
Because he wanted a blazer.

WHO PUT HIS TELEVISION SET IN THE OVEN?
He wanted a TV dinner.

WHO TRIED TO GET A NO CLAIMS BONUS ON HIS LIFE INSURANCE?

WHO CHEATED CIE?
He bought a return ticket to Dublin and never went back.

WHO DAMAGED HIS HEALTH DRINKING MILK?
The cow fell on him.

WHO COULDN'T UNDERSTAND HOW PEOPLE ALWAYS SEEMED TO DIE IN ALPHABETICAL ORDER?

OUTSIDE A KERRY GARAGE

> **OUR ATTENDANTS ARE FILLING FINE TANK YOU**

CROSSWORDS FOR KERRYMEN

1 ACROSS THE SIXTEENTH LETTER OF THE ALPHABET

1 DOWN PARKING ALLOWED.

1 ACROSS MYSELF (ANAGRAM)
1 DOWN THE NINTH LETTER OF THE ALPHABET

LAST WEEK'S SOLUTION
[CLUES ON REQUEST]
THERE WERE NO CORRECT ENTRIES PRIZE OF £1 DIVIDED EQUALLY AMONG 5317 PEOPLE WHO SUBMITTED THE SOLUTION WITH THE LEAST NUMBER OF MISTAKES.

EASY CROSSWORD

First Kerry snake: 'Are we a poisonous variety of snakes?'
Second Kerry snake: 'I don't know. Why do you ask?'
First Kerry snake: 'I've just bitten my tongue.'

Have you heard about the Kerry stork?
He used to deliver butter to maternity hospitals.

Two Kerrymen joined the Army during the Second World War and were fighting in the trenches for the first time. To encourage them, their sergeant promised them a pound for every German they killed. One afternoon one of them was woken up from his nap by the other shouting, 'They're coming, they're coming.'
'Who's coming?' said the other.
'The Germans, that's who.'
'How many are there?'
'About a hundred thousand.'
'Begorra,' said the Kerryman reaching for his rifle, 'our fortune's made.'

A Kerryman was walking through a field one day when he spotted a leprechaun so he captured him and demanded three wishes.
'Right,' said the leprechaun, 'what's your first wish?'
'I'd like a purse full of gold,' said the Kerryman, 'that no matter how much you take out of it, it will never be empty.'
'Right,' said the leprechaun and gave it to him.
The Kerryman grabbed it and tried it out and was delighted to see that it worked.
'For my second and third wishes, I'll have two more of those purses '

Have you heard about the Kerryman's pet mosquito?
It was so tame it used to eat out of his hand.

Comment at a Kerry funeral: If that man was alive today, he'd turn in his grave to see some of the people who turned up at his funeral.

HOW MANY KERRYMEN DOES IT TAKE

TO LAUNCH A SHIP?
1001 — One to hold the bottle of champagne and a thousand to bang the ship against it.

TO MILK A COW?
24 — One to hold each teat and twenty to lift the cow up and down.

TO HANG A PICTURE?
30 — One to hold the picture, one to hold the screw and twenty-eight to turn the wall around.

TO CHANGE A LIGHT BULB?
100 — One to actually change the light bulb and ninety-nine to share the experience.

TO CARRY OUT A KIDNAPPING?
Ten — One to capture the kid and nine to write the ransom note.

TO WASH AN UPSTAIRS WINDOW?
Two — One to wash the window, one to hold the ladder.

TO WASH A DOWNSTAIRS WINDOW?
Four — One to wash the window, one to hold the ladder and two to dig a hole for the ladder.

TWO SIGNS ON THE SAME POLE SEEN IN KERRY

GENTLEMEN'S TOILET ⟶

LIMIT TWO TONS

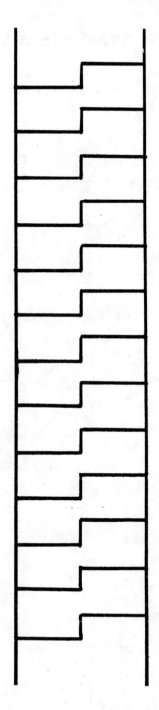

LADDER FOR A KERRYMAN WITH A LIMP

THE KINGDOM STRIKES BACK

WHY ARE CORKMEN SO CONSTIPATED?
They hate to part with *ANYTHING*.

WHY DO CLAREMEN HAVE SCRATCHED FACES?
From trying to eat with knives and forks.

WHAT DO YOU GET IF YOU CROSS A SLIGOMAN WITH A GORILLA?
A mentally deficient gorilla.

WHY DID THE MAYO FISHERMAN STAY UNMARRIED?
He couldn't find a girl who had worms.

WHAT DO YOU GET IF YOU CROSS A DUBLINER WITH A BOOMERANG?
A dirty smell you can't get rid of.

WHAT DO YOU CALL A CORKMAN WHO MARRIES A GORILLA?
A social climber.

HOW DO YOU BRAINWASH A TIPPERARYMAN?
Fill his wellingtons with water.

WHAT DO YOU CALL A PIMPLE ON A KILKENNYMAN'S REAR END?
A brain tumour.

HAVE YOU HEARD ABOUT THE MAYOMAN WHO HAD A BRAIN TRANSPLANT?
The brain rejected him.

SOME KERRY INVENTIONS

A cure for wheatgerm

Non-stick glue

A new way to keep you from losing your hair
— sew a name tag inside your hairpiece

A new CURE FOR HICCUPS
— hold your breath and count to a million

Motorway bowling

The crossed line
— invented by Alexander Graham Sheehy

A Hernia transplant

An out-patient morgue

DEHYDRATED WATER
for desert explorers

A washing machine for disposable nappies

The MILLION POUND SWEEPSTAKE
— one pound to the winner
every year for a million years

A FOOLPROOF WAY OF AVOIDING PARKING TICKETS
— take the windscreen wipers off your car

Green Golf Balls

HAVE YOU HEARD ABOUT THE KERRYMAN

WHO NEVER BOUGHT A SUIT WITH TWO PAIRS OF TROUSERS?
He felt too hot wearing two pairs of trousers.

WHO SWALLOWED A PILLOW?
He felt a little down in the mouth.

WHO GOT 100% IN HIS EXAM?
20% in English; 30% in Irish; 40% in mathematics; 10% VAT.

WHO HAD A DRINK PROBLEM?
He couldn't afford all he was drinking.

WHO BOUGHT A CARPET IN MINT CONDITION?
It had a hole in the middle.

WHO STAYED UP ALL NIGHT STUDYING FOR A BLOOD TEST?

WHO GOT A NEW BOOMERANG FOR CHRISTMAS?
It took him six months to throw his old one away.

WHO WENT TO A DRIVE-IN MOVIE TO WATCH THE FILM?

WHO THOUGHT THE CHARGE OF THE LIGHT BRIGADE WAS HIS ESB BILL?

WHO THOUGHT FREE SPEECH MEANT NOT HAVING TO PAY YOUR TELEPHONE BILL?

WHO WROTE A FIRST-CLASS NOVEL?
You know the way the kids write in first class!

WHO CAME HOME ONE NIGHT AND FOUND HIS HOUSE LOCKED?
He borrowed a ladder, climbed in an upstairs window and found a note from his wife in the kitchen saying, 'The key is under the doormat and your salad is in the oven.'

WHO WENT TO A FIRE SALE AND BOUGHT A FIRE?

WHO WROTE TO THE INCOME TAX PEOPLE AND TOLD THEM HE DIDN'T WANT TO JOIN THEIR CLUB?

WHO PUT A PACKET OF DAZ ON HIS TELEVISION SET BECAUSE HE DIDN'T HAVE ANY ARIEL?

WHO TOOK NOTHING FOR A HEADACHE BECAUSE HE HEARD THAT NOTHING ACTS FASTER THAN ANADIN?

WHO HIJACKED A SUBMARINE?
He demanded a million pounds ransom and a parachute.

HAVE YOU HEARD ABOUT THE KERRYMAN WHO THOUGHT

CYCLAMATES were a husband and wife on a tandem?

HARD WATER was another name for ice?

CHAMPAGNE was French for 'false window?'

THE ENGLISH CHANNEL was BBC television?

JOHNNY CASH was a sort of pay toilet?

That if he fell in love he would lose his appetite?
He was right — for tea he used to have eighteen slices of bread;
now he only eats seventeen.

RADIO ACTIVITY was what went on in RTE?

FOR LETTERS TOO LATE FOR THE NEXT DELIVERY

SIGN BY A POSTBOX IN A KERRY POST OFFICE

THICKSILVER

What's the difference between electricity and lightning?
YOU HAVE TO PAY FOR ELECTRICITY.

In astronomy what's another name for a star with a tail?
MICKEY MOUSE.

How do you tell the difference between a baby boy and a baby girl?
A BABY BOY WEARS BLUE BOOTEES AND A BABY GIRL WEARS
PINK BOOTEES.

How do you tell the difference between a toadstool and a mushroom?
EAT IT — IF YOU DIE IT'S A TOADSTOOL AND IF YOU LIVE IT'S A
MUSHROOM .

What's the connection between 1916 and 1798?
ADJOINING ROOMS IN A KERRY HOTEL.

What are your parent's names? MAMMA AND DADDA

Why do storks have such long legs?
IF THEIR LEGS WERE ANY SHORTER THEY WOULDN'T REACH
THE GROUND.

How do you spell 'Tipperary'?
DO YOU MEAN THE TOWN NOW OR THE COUNTY?

What do you call a male bee? A WASP.

What is the Ayatullah famous for?
HE FOUNDED THE CEILÍ BAND.

Who was the mythical creature, half man, half beast? BUFFALO BILL .

What rugby player has been capped most times for Ireland?
A. N. OTHER.

An important businessman was staying in a little Kerry hotel and the receptionist asked him if he would like a call in the morning.
'Certainly not,' he snapped. 'I wake at seven o'clock sharp every morning.'
'In that case,' said the receptionist, 'would you mind calling the porter?'

A Kerryman bought one of the fantastic new Japanese mini bubble cars but it didn't work out very well.
Dogs kept wetting the windows.

A Kerryman fell into shark-infested waters but survived because he was wearing a T-shirt with *CORK FOR THE SAM MAGUIRE CUP* on it — not even the sharks would swallow that.

A Kerryman went into a butcher's shop and saw an electric fan in its protective wire grill for the first time.
'That's a very lively bird you have in that cage,' he said to the butcher.

Have you heard about the Kerry beggarman who was standing at a street corner with a hat in each hand?
Business was so good he explained that he had opened a branch office.

A Kerryman was being tried on a serious offence.
'You say you left the country in 1976,' said the prosecuting counsel, 'and returned in 1979. What were you doing in the interim?'
'Never set foot in the place,' said the Kerryman.

A Kerryman owned an optician's shop and one Friday afternoon at about a minute to closing time a fellow walked in with a broken pair of glasses and asked if they could be fixed as he needed them for the weekend.
'Sorry,' said the Kerryman, 'we're just closing but I could board them up for you until Monday.'

A Kerryman was doing a test to become a policeman.
'How far is it from Cork to Dublin?' he was asked.
'I don't know,' said the Kerryman, 'but if that's going to be my beat, I don't want the job.'

SOME KERRY LANDSCAPES

MIDNIGHT ON BALLYBUNION BEACH

A BLACKOUT IN KILLARNEY

A PHOTOGRAPHIC DARKROOM IN TRALEE

HAVE YOU HEARD ABOUT THE KERRYMAN WHO THOUGHT –

MANUAL LABOUR was a Spanish trade union official?

SLIM PANATELLA was a country and western singer?

CHOU-EN-LAI was Chinese for bed and breakfast?

YOKO ONO was Japanese for one egg please?

A DISCOTEQUE was a Cork traffic warden?

A METRONOME was a dwarf who lived in the Paris underground?

A STALAGMITE was a midget who lived in a German concentration camp?

COPPER NITRATE was overtime pay for policemen?

HERTZ VAN RENTAL was a Dutch artist?

A P.45 was a revolver?

PAS DE DEUX was French for father of twins?

FRENCH COALMEN DELIVERED COAL-DE-SACK OR À LA CART?

ON A KERRY OPTICIANS

> **IF YOU CAN'T READ THIS NOTICE
> COME IN AND HAVE YOUR EYES TESTED
> — YOU MAY NEED GLASSES**

Have you heard about the ship that set sail from Kerry with a cargo of yo-yos? It sank two hundred and thirty-seven times.

Two Kerrymen were boasting to each other how dumb their sons were.
'Let me show you how bad my son Mick is,' said the first. 'Come here Mick,' he said, calling him in. 'Here's a pound, now go into town and buy me a Rolls Royce.' Off went Mick to town.

'That's nothing,' said the second Kerryman. 'Wait until you see my son Dinny. Come here Dinny; now go into town to Sullivans' pub and see if I'm there.' So off went Dinny.

On the way to town Mick and Dinny met and began to boast about how dumb their fathers were.

'Take my old man,' said Mick. 'He's just sent me into town with a pound to buy a Rolls Royce, and every fool knows the salesrooms are closed today.'

'That's nothing,' said Dinny. 'My old man is really the limit. He's just sent me into Sullivans' pub to see if he's there. Couldn't he have just picked up the phone by his elbow and found out for himself in a second?'

A rather mean tourist arrived up in Kerry and asked if he could have a bed for the night for £2.
'Right,' said a Kerry hotelier, anxious to please.
'If I give you another 50p will you throw in breakfast as well?' asked the skin-flint.
'Right,' said the Kerryman, raising his eyes to Heaven.
At about six o'clock in the morning the tourist was awakened by the door opening suddenly and a loud thump on the floor.
'What was that?' he cried in alarm.
'Breakfast being thrown in,' smiled the Kerryman.

Have you heard about the Kerryman who was sentenced to transportation for life in Tasmania in 1773? He came to a sticky end because he tried to tunnel his way out of the prison ship.

A Corkman holidaying in Kerry lost his Post Office Savings book. A few weeks later it was handed to the Gardai with £500 extra deposited in it.

THE KINGDOM STRIKES BACK

How do you break an OFFALYMAN'S finger?
Kick him in the nose.

What's the most popular kind of marmalade sold in WATERFORD?
Thick cut.

Newspaper Headline — *BED COLLAPSES IN SUNDAY'S WELL — 43 CORKMEN HURT.*

Where do Kerry babies come from?
You don't know? And you think Kerrymen are dumb!

The EEC has just given £1000 million to build three new looney bins. One is in Rome, one is in Brussels and **they're putting a roof over Dublin.**

What's the world's thinnest book?
The Book of Carlow Intellectuals.

Have you heard about the raffle where first prize was a week in Longford and second prize was two weeks in LONGFORD?

What does a LOUTHMAN think when he gets diarrhoea?
He thinks he's melting.

How do you know if a WICKLOWMAN is in love?
If he washes his feet more often than once a month.

What's the difference between a WEXFORDMAN and a bucket of manure?
The bucket.

How do you save a GALWAYMAN from drowning?
You don't know?
Good.

Have you heard about the LIMERICKMAN who thought he was a great wit?
He was half right.

What's the latest thing in air pollution?
The Roscommon parachute club.

Have you heard about the CORK GOALKEEPER who was so depressed after a six-goal defeat by Kerry that he threw himself under a bus?
He missed and the bus went under his body.

What do you call a DEAD DUBLINER?
A jack in the box.

What did God say when he made his second MEATHMAN?
Gee, I must be losing my touch.

How do you tell the age of a CAVANMAN?
Cut off his head and count the rings.

What's the difference between a MAYOMAN and a ham sandwich?
A ham sandwich is only half an inch thick.

How do you keep LEITRIM MEN out of your house?
Hide the key under a bar of soap.

How do you recognise a Kerryman in Croke Park?
He's the one holding the Sam Maguire cup!

What do you call an intelligent MAYOMAN?
Very, very lucky.

Why do TIPPERARYMEN always carry a little rubbish in their pockets?
Identification.

Have you heard about the CORKMAN who had an inferiority complex?
He thought other people were nearly as good as he was.

What's the difference between a DUBLIN wedding and a DUBLIN wake?
One less drunk.

A Kerryman had a clever little dog that he took to the Munster football final each year. After the match the dog would bark out Kerry's winning score and clap his little paws together. A reporter from the *Cork Examiner* asked him what the dog did when Cork won.
'I don't know,' said the Kerryman, 'I've only had him ten years.'

What's blue and white and slides down the table?
The Dublin football team.

Why is the wheelbarrow the greatest of all man's inventions?
It taught Dubliners to walk on their hind legs.

Why do DONEGALMEN have big noses?
Donegalmen have such big fingers.

What is gross ignorance?
144 Corkmen.

What does a CLAREMAN do when he stops drinking?
He belches.

Why are Kerrymen jokes so simple?
So MAYOMEN can understand them.

What's blue and white and floats upside down in the Liffey?
A Dubliner caught telling Kerryman jokes.

What's a CORK barbeque?
A fire in a garbage pail.

WHAT DO YOU CALL

A Kerryman chasing a garbage truck?
A GALLOPING GOURMET.

A Kerry garda sitting up a tree?
A SPECIAL BRANCH MAN.

A Kerryman with a Cork accent?
A SOCIAL CLIMBER.

A Kerryman under a wheelbarrow?
A MECHANIC.

A Kerryman who rides his bicycle on the pavement?
A PSYCHOPATH.

A Kerryman travelling to Cork with a wheelbarrow?
A THRILL-SEEKER.

A Brick on a Kerryman's head?
AN EXTENSION.

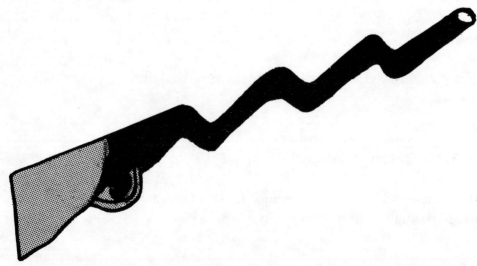

A GUN FOR SHOOTING KERRY KANGAROOS

A Kerryman told his little boy to go down to the chemist shop and buy half a pound of cockroach powder. 'But,' he warned him, 'don't let on to the chemist what it's for.'
The little boy bought the powder and then asked the chemist, 'Is this stuff good for cockroaches?'
'No,' said the chemist, 'It kills them stone dead.'

A Kerryman once claimed that Kerry had the best climate in the country except for the fact that the weather ruined it.

The first time a Kerryman saw a toupee in a shop window he said, 'Isn't it amazing how they can get hair to grow on that thing but not on your head.'

Have you heard about the Kerry snake?
He fell in love with a coil of rope.

A Kerry priest was preaching to his congregation in the middle of the last century.
'Drink is the cause of all your problems,' he thundered.
'It makes you angry, it makes you hate your landlords, it makes you shoot at your landlords, and worst of all, it makes you miss.'

A West Cork farmer went to a fair in Kerry with his beautiful ivory handled whip, whose name he pronounced 'Wup'. However, he lost his wup and was going from pub to pub asking everyone if anybody had seen his wup. In one pub one little Kerryman nudged another and said, 'Did oo hear fwat he called his fip?'

If a Kerryman dials a wrong number what does he say to the person who answers the phone?
'You fool you've got the wrong number.'

A Kerryman was kissing his girlfriend passionately when her father suddenly burst into the room.
He grabbed the Kerryman by the throat and shouted, 'What were you doing to my daughter?'
'I was only whispering into her mouth, sir,' said the Kerryman.

HOW DO YOU RECOGNISE

A KERRYMAN ON AN OIL-RIG?
He's the one throwing crusts of bread to the helicopters.

A KERRYMAN SANTA CLAUS?
He's carrying a bag of Easter eggs.

A FORGED KERRY £1 NOTE?
Look for the words 'illegal tender'.

A KERRY ZEBRA?
He's called 'Spot'.

A KERRYMAN IN A CAR-WASH?
He's the one sitting on his motor-bike.

A KERRY CAMEL?
He's always thirsty.

A KERRY WOODWORM?
He's dead on top of a brick.

A KERRY FORMULA ONE DRIVER?
He makes a hundred pit stops — three for fuel, four for tyre changes and ninety-three to ask for directions.

A WELL MANNERED KERRYMAN?
He doesn't blow his soup — he fans it with his cap.

A KERRYMAN'S TOILET ROLL?
Look for the instructions printed on every sheet.

IN A KERRY CHURCH

> **CLOSED ON**
> **SUNDAYS**

During the recent petrol crisis a Kerryman was charged with syphoning the air out of the tyres of a car.
Clever Kerrymen however survived the crisis by putting a brick in their petrol tank.

Have you heard about the Kerry hedgehog?
It fell in love with a hairbrush.

A Kerryman got a job as a doorman in a big building. He managed very well with the PUSH and PULL signs but he was seen struggling with his fingers under a door marked LIFT.

A Kerryman was captain of a jet and one day he made the following announcement to his passengers over the public address system.
    'Ladies and gentlemen, sorry for the long delay in take off. I'm delighted to announce that we haven't got a bomb on board as we first feared. At least, if we have, we haven't been able to find it.

A Kerry terrorist was being tried by a kangaroo court on the charge of betraying the organisation. The entire proceedings were conducted through the medium of Irish. Said the Kerryman to the judge, *'Ceapann tusa anois gur spaire Sasanach mise.'*
'Ní cheapaim,' said the judge, so they did.

A Kerryman got a job as a chauffeur to a duchess and gave every satisfaction as a driver. However, she noticed that he was a little careless about his appearance and in particular that he didn't seem to shave every day, so she decided to drop a few hints.
'James,' she said one morning to him casually, 'how often do you think one should shave?'
'Well ma'am,' he replied slowly, 'with a light growth like yours, I'd say about once every three days.'

A Kerryman was asked to join the Save Energy campaign by not carrying heavy, unnecessary weights in the boot of his car. He decided to leave his car jack at home because he didn't use it very often.

HAVE YOU HEARD ABOUT THE KERRYMAN

Who became a tap dancer?
He got washed down the sink.

Who tried to iron his curtains?
He fell out the window.

Who took his trousers off when the doctor told him to strip to the waist?

Who claimed he caught a fish so big that the photograph alone weighed twenty pounds?

Who sent his kids to a school for emotionally disturbed teachers?

Who wasn't superstitious in case it brought him bad luck?

Who got a pair of cuff links for Christmas?
He had his wrists pierced.

Who had only three children because he heard that every fourth child born is Chinese?

Who failed to get into the Gardaí because the minimum height was 5'-8" and he was 5'-9"?

Who thought that publishers had entered into a conspiracy against him because twenty of them returned the manuscript of his first novel?

Who refused to pay going into the art gallery because he was only looking?

IN A KERRY DANCE HALL

> **LADIES AND GENTLEMEN WELCOME**
> **REGARDLESS OF SEX**

A Kerryman was in charge of a hospital for the disabled and one day he was showing a millionaire round the place in the hope of getting a large donation from him. So he took him into a ward where there was a man with no arms. 'That's dreadful,' said the millionaire. 'Look, here's a cheque for £50,000.' The Kerryman thought he would squeeze a little more money out of him, so he took him into a ward where there was a man with neither arms nor legs. 'That's terrible,' said the millionaire. 'I'll increase that to £100,000.' The Kerryman decided to squeeze just a little more money out of his bene- factor, so he took him to a ward where there was a bed with just a single tooth lying on the pillow. 'Oh my God,' gasped the millionaire, 'is that all that's left of the poor fellow?' 'Worse still,' said the Kerryman, 'he's having it out tomorrow.'

A Kerryman went to the doctor to get some medicine as he wasn't feeling very well. 'This is pretty strong stuff,' said the doctor, 'so take some the first day, then skip a day, take some again and then skip another day and so on.' A few months later the doctor met the Kerryman's wife and asked her how he was. 'Oh he's dead,' she told him. 'Didn't the medicine I prescribed do him any good?' asked the doctor. 'Oh the medicine was fine,' she replied. 'It was all that skipping that killed him.'

What does a Kerryman think when he sees his underarm hair? He thinks the stuffing is coming out.

A Kerryman was drinking too much, so his local Parish Priest persuaded him to join the Pioneer Total Abstinence Association. About a week later the Parish Priest observed the Kerryman staggering out of a pub. 'I thought you were a pioneer now,' said the Parish Priest. 'I am,' said the Kerryman, 'but not a bigoted one.'

Why are there so many great Kerry pianists and so few great Kerry violinists? Have you ever tried balancing a pint of porter on a violin?

HAVE YOU HEARD ABOUT THE KERRYMAN WHO THOUGHT

TONIC SOLFA was something you put in a drink?

A SPIRIT LEVEL was a breathalyser for carpenters?

VAT 69 was the Pope's telephone number?

BACTERIA was the rear entrance to a café?

ET CUM SPIRITU 20 was the Bishop of Dublin's telephone number?

CAPITAL PUNISHMENT meant living in Dublin?

SHERLOCK HOLMES was a block of flats?

AN INNUENDO was an Italian suppository?

INTERPOL would send a parrot abroad for you?

A BARBECUE was a line of people outside a hairdressers?

THE AAAA was an association for drunks who drive?
So he joined and when he got drunk he rang them up and they towed him away from the bar.

SYNTAX was money paid to the government by wrongdoers?

COQ AU VIN was chicken that fell off the back of a lorry?

PLATO was a Greek washing-up liquid?

IN A KERRY NEWSPAPER

> **PASSPORT FOR SALE:**
> **OWNER GOING ABROAD**

THE KINGDOM STRIKES BACK

WHY DO DUBLINERS KEEP THEIR MOUTHS OPEN ALL THE TIME?
They're so lazy it saves them having to open their mouths when they want to yawn.

HOW DO YOU GET FORTY CORKMEN INTO A MINI?
Tell them it's going to Dublin.

HOW DO YOU GET THEM OUT AGAIN?
Tell them they're sharing the petrol.

WHAT IS BLACK AND FRIZZLED AND HANGS FROM THE CEILING?
A Galway electrician.

HOW DOES A DUBLINER KEEP FLIES OUT OF HIS KITCHEN?
He dumps a load of manure in his living room.

WHY DO BIRDS FLY UPSIDE DOWN OVER KERRY?
To save all they've got for Cork.

HOW DO YOU KNOW IF A MEATHMAN IS LYING?
If his lips are moving.

HAVE YOU HEARD ABOUT THE CORKMAN WHO WAS WRONG ONLY ONCE IN HIS LIFE?
That's when he thought he had made a mistake.

WHAT'S THE DIFFERENCE BETWEEN A KILDAREMAN AND HIS PHOTOGRAPH?
The photograph is fully developed.

SOLITAIRE NAUGHTS AND CROSSES

O	O	O
O	O	O
O	O	O

Have you heard about the Kerryman who got sick all over the floor of a Dublin art gallery?
He was offered £35,000 for it.

How do you recognise a Kerryman in Las Vegas?
He's the one playing the stamp machine.

A Kerryman was boasting about the ring he had bought for his wife.
'It's got four diamonds, three rubies and half a dozen sapphires. . . missing.'

A Kerryman went into a bar with two sophisticated friends.
'I'll have a Martini,' said the first, 'with an olive in it please.'
'I'll have a brandy,' said the second, ' and put a cherry in it please.'
'I'll have a pint of porter,' said the Kerryman, 'and put an onion in it.'

Have you heard about the Kerryman who got a job as a teabag drier for CIE?

How do you recognise a Kerryman's best socks?
The one with fewest holes.

A Kerryman was asked how many honours he had obtained in his Leaving Cert.
'Three,' he replied, 'Applied Mathematics and Pure Mathematics.'

Have you heard about the Kerryman who returned to Ireland during the famine to open a fish and chip shop?

Two Kerrymen were out walking together when they saw a lorry pass by laden with grassy sods of earth for the laying of a lawn.
'Do you know Mick,' said one of them to the other, 'if I ever get rich that's what I'll have done — send away my lawn to be cut.'

KERRY ROAD SIGN

**THIS IS THE WRONG ROAD TO DUBLIN
DO NOT TAKE THIS ROAD**

IN A KERRY SHOP

**NO DISSATISFIED CUSTOMER
IS EVER ALLOWED TO LEAVE
THIS SHOP**

A KERRY CUSTOMER IN A SELF—SERVICE PETROL STATION

A Kerry barman was closing up one night when he found a customer flat out under a table so he propped him up against the bar. When he turned round he found the fellow had slid onto the floor again so he picked him up, searched his pockets and found his name and address. So he put him in his car, drove him home, and carried him up to the front door. To ring the doorbell, he propped him up against the wall and found that he again slid down on the ground. As he tried to lift him up again, the fellow's wife opened the door and said, 'Oh thank goodness you've brought him home — but where's his wheelchair?'

In a little Kerry village the coroner was summing up in a suicide case before a jury of twelve Kerrymen.
'If you believe beyond reasonable doubt,' he told them, 'that the deceased did shoot himself with a gun, then it is your duty in law to return a verdict of *felo de se.*'
   The jury was out about four hours and when they returned the foreman said, 'We agree that the deceased did shoot himself with a gun, but if the coroner claims he fell in the sea we return a verdict of accidentally drowned.'

Have you heard about the Kerry addict who quit the drug scene?
He tried sniffing coke but the bubbles kept going up his nose.

A Kerryman went for an X-ray and was immediately rushed to hospital for a hole-in-the-heart operation. Then they discovered it was only a Polo Mint in his shirt pocket.

Two American ladies had just been driven round the Lakes of Killarney by a silver-tongued little jarvey for over four hours. As they paid him they said, 'We'd love to give you a tip but there is a notice on your jaunting car saying TIPPING FORBIDDEN.'
'God help your sense,' smiled the Kerryman, 'TIPPING FORBIDDEN! So was eating apples in the Garden of Eden.'

A Kerryman was in court charged with parking his car in a restricted area. The judge asked him if he had anything to say in his defence.
'They shouldn't put up such misleading notices,' said the Kerryman, 'It said FINE FOR PARKING HERE.'

HOW DOES A KERRYMAN

FORGE 10p PIECES?
He cuts the corners off 50p pieces.

AMUSE HIMSELF?
He writes P.T.O. on both sides of a piece of paper.

MAKE A VENETIAN BLIND?
He throws acid in his eyes.

MAKE ANTI-FREEZE?
He hides her woollen nightie.

MAKE AN OLD GERMAN WHINE?
He stands on his toe.

MAKE A SWISS ROLL?
He pushes him down the Alps.

MAKE A MALTESE CROSS?
He bites his finger.

CURE WATER ON THE BRAIN?
With a tap on the head.

CURE WATER ON THE KNEE?
With pumps and drainpipe trousers.

TEAR A TELEPHONE DIRECTORY IN TWO?

Page by page.

Have you heard about the Kerry boxer who never won any of his fights? Every time an opponent knocked him down he remembered what his mother had told him so he counted to ten before getting up and hitting him back.

A Kerryman went into a bar and the barman said, 'What are you having sir?' 'Thank you very much,' said the Kerryman, 'I'll have a pint.' So the barman pulled him a pint and asked for the appropriate amount of money.
'Hold on,' said the Kerryman. 'You asked me what I was having, so this should be a free drink.'
'Get out of here,' said the barman angrily, 'and don't come back.'
About a month later the Kerryman walked into the same bar with the same barman behind the counter.
'Look,' said the barman, 'I thought I told you to get out and stay out.'
'That's a nice way to treat a new customer,' said the Kerryman, 'I've never been in here in my life before.'
'I'm terribly sorry sir,' said the barman, 'I mistook you for someone who looks remarkably like you — you must have a double.'
'Certainly,' said the Kerryman, 'I'll have a double brandy.'

A Kerryman went to Confession and confessed his sins.
'You are forgiven,' said the priest. 'Now for your penance say three Hail Marys.'
'But I only know one,' said the Kerryman.

A Kerryman got a job in a big house as a servant but one afternoon he knocked over a priceless Ming vase and broke it into little pieces.
'Good Heavens,' said his employer, 'do you realise what you have done? That vase was over a thousand years old.'
'Thank goodness,' said the Kerryman, 'it wasn't a new one.'

Members wanted by the Kerry Fencing Club — new blood is always welcome.

How do you know if there is a sale on in a Kerry shop?
Look for signs such as *WAS £13.99 — NOW ONLY £15.*

Have you heard about the Kerryman who went into a drapers shop and asked for some of the new terminal underwear?

CAUSES OF DEATH
ON SOME KERRY DEATH CERTIFICATES

HE DIDN'T DIE OF ANYTHING SERIOUS

HAD NEVER BEEN FATALLY ILL BEFORE

CAUSE OF DEATH UNKNOWN
AS HE DIED WITHOUT THE AID OF A DOCTOR

WENT TO BED FEELING VERY WELL BUT WOKE UP DEAD

AN ACT OF GOD UNDER VERY SUSPICIOUS CIRCUMSTANCES

[OF A HATED LANDLORD FOUND WITH TWENTY BULLET
WOUNDS
(TEN FATAL, TEN NON-FATAL)]
— LEAD POISONING

HE DIED OF A TUESDAY

THE PATIENT DIED IN A STATE OF PERFECT HEALTH

[OF A MAN FOUND DEAD WITH THIRTY STAB WOUNDS
AND TWENTY BULLET WOUNDS]
— THE WORST CASE OF SUICIDE EVER SEEN IN THE COUNTRY

HERE LIES
THE BODY OF
LT. COL. MACMAHON
ACCIDENTALLY SHOT
BY HIS BATMAN
WHILE CLEANING
HIS RIFLE
'WELL DONE THOU GOOD
AND FAITHFUL SERVANT.'

Have you heard about the Kerryman who set out to walk around the world?
He was drowned just off Valentia Island.

Two Kerrymen went to South America where they got caught up in a revolution. They were captured and sentenced to death by firing squad. As they were about to be shot, one of them asked for a blindfold but was refused.
'How come,' he protested, 'that the two fellows who were shot just before us were given blindfolds?'
'Look,' said the other Kerryman, 'don't make trouble.'

An old Kerry Army sergeant wasn't feeling very well so he went to the doctor and had a check-up.
'When did you last have a drink,' the doctor asked him. '1945,' said the Kerryman.
'That's a long time without a drink,' said the doctor.
'It certainly is,' said the Kerryman, 'It's nearly 2130 now.'

Have you heard about the Kerryman who invented a new shockproof, waterproof, rustproof watch?
It was for people who wanted to tell the time when they were drowning.

Have you heard about the Kerryman charged with breaking into Árus An Uachtaráin?
He gave himself away by signing the Visitors' Book.

A Kerryman was a lighthouse-keeper for forty years and every hour on the hour a big bell on the lighthouse rang out the time. One night he went to bed at midnight having heard the clock ring out twelve times. He went to sleep but at one o'clock the bell failed to ring, and there was complete silence. The Kerryman sat bolt upright in his bed and said, 'What was that?'

Have you heard about the Kerryman who became a hero when his house was flooded?
He went back in to rescue the goldfish.

A Kerryman had a severe pain in his head so he went to the doctor who examined his brain. But the doctor found nothing.

WHY

DO KERRY DOGS HAVE FLAT FACES?
From chasing parked cars.

DO YOU NEVER GET ICE IN YOUR DRINK IN KERRY?
The fellow with the recipe emigrated.

DO KERRY FISH SWIM BACKWARDS?
To keep the water from getting into their eyes.

DOES A KERRYMAN SMILE WHEN STRUCK BY LIGHTNING?
He thinks he's having his photograph taken.

DID THE KERRYMAN PUT HIS WIFE UNDER THE BED?
He thought she was a little potty.

DO KERRYMEN SMILE SO MUCH?
Their false teeth are too big for them.

DOES A KERRYMAN READ THE OBITUARY COLUMN IN HIS NEWSPAPER EVERY MORNING?
To see if he's still alive.

DO KERRYMEN NEVER MENTION THE NUMBER 288?
It's too gross.

DO KERRY WORKERS NEVER GET TEA BREAKS?
It takes too long to retrain them afterwards.

DO KERRYMEN MAKE POOR CARDPLAYERS?
Every time they pick up a spade they spit on their hands.

ON A KERRY RESTAURANT

> **CLOSED**
> **FOR LUNCH**

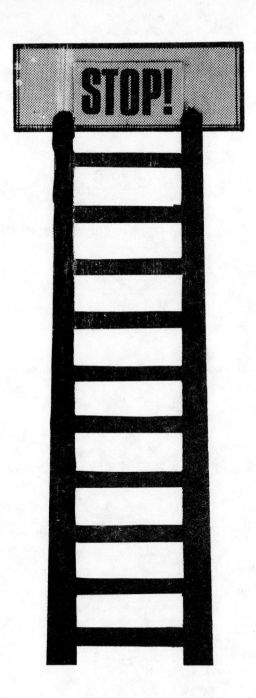

A KERRY LADDER

How do you recognise a bathing suit made in Kerry?
Look for the label which says *DRY CLEAN ONLY*.

An Irish-speaking Kerryman went to Iran where he was being questioned about his political opinions.
'Do you support the Ayatollah?' they asked him.
'Sea,' he replied, so they shot him.

Two Kerrymen joined the RAF during the Second World War and were sent on a mission to drop bombs over Germany. As they flew over Berlin they were met by a burst of anti-aircraft guns, machine guns and chased by German aircraft.
At the height of the action one of the Kerrymen shouted out 'Hurrah for De Valera.'
'Why on earth are you shouting out that?' asked the other Kerryman.
'Wasn't it him that kept us out of the war?' said the first Kerryman.

A tourist called at a hotel owned by a Kerryman and asked what his weekly rates were.
'I don't know,' said the Kerryman, 'nobody has ever stayed that long.'

How do you recognise a Kerryman in a bus?
He's the one sitting in the back seat because he thinks he's getting a longer ride.

A Kerryman's shop was burgled one night so he called the police.
'Thank goodness it wasn't last week it happened,' he said to a policeman.
'Why is that, sir?' asked the policeman.
'Well,' said the Kerryman, 'I'd have lost a colossal amount of money; but this week I was having a sale and everything was marked down 50%.'

OUTSIDE A KERRY BARBERS

SPECIAL OFFER
HAIRCUTS 50p THIS WEEK ONLY
ONE PER CUSTOMER ONLY

A Kerryman's cat was feeling out of sorts so he called in the vet.
'There's nothing really the matter with your cat', said the vet. 'It's all perfectly natural, she's going to have kittens.'
'That's impossible,' said the Kerryman, 'she's a prizewinning cat and I've never let her out of my sight for a moment. She's never been near a tom cat in her life.'
'How about him over there?' asked the vet, pointing to a big tom cat sitting on a couch smiling to himself.
'Don't be ridiculous,' said the Kerryman, 'that's her brother.'

From the newspapers: WANTED URGENTLY — NEW MEMBERS FOR A SUICIDE CLUB IN THE KERRY AREA.

How do you sell a twenty pound hammer to a Kerryman?
Tell him it costs only ten pounds.

Have you heard about the latest Kerry invention?
It's a digital sun dial.

A customer went into a shop owned by a Kerryman and asked to buy some mustard.
'I don't have any in the shop,' said the Kerryman, 'but I have some in the store; come with me and pick out the kind of mustard you want.'
As they went through the store the customer couldn't help noticing bag after bag of salt on the shelves.
'You must sell an awful lot of salt,' he remarked to the Kerryman.
'I sell very little salt,' said the Kerryman, 'but the fellow who sells me salt, boy, can he sell salt.'

Have you heard about the Kerryman who got rid of his vacuum cleaner because he felt it was only gathering dust?

Have you heard about the Kerryman who took a speed-reading course?
The first book he read afterwards was *War and Peace* and when asked what it was about he replied, 'It's about Russia.'

HOW DO YOU RECOGNISE

A KERRYMAN WHO OWNS A VOLKSWAGEN?
He has a fifteen foot starting handle.

A KERRYMAN'S CENTRAL HEATING SYSTEM?
Lagging jackets on the radiators.

A KERRY RACING CYCLIST?
Stabilisers on his bicycle.

A KERRY PHYSICAL FITNESS FANATIC?
He rolls his own cigarettes.

A PASSIONATE KERRYMAN?
He takes the cigarette out of his mouth when kissing a girl.

A KERRYMAN'S CORDLESS RAZOR?
A piece of sandpaper.

A KERRY MUGGER?
He gives his victims business cards in case they are ever in the neighbourhood again.

A KERRY TORTOISE?
His shell has been recalled.

A KERRY WATER SKIER?
He's being towed by a rowboat.

KERRY IDENTICAL TWINS?
They can't tell each other apart.

IN A KERRY POST OFFICE

**PENS WILL NOT BE PROVIDED UNTIL PEOPLE
STOP TAKING THEM AWAY**

A fellow went into a shop owned by a Kerryman and asked for some toilet paper.

'Sorry,' said the Kerryman, 'we have no summer novelties in stock at the moment.'

There's a fantastic new act that's going down very well on the cabaret scene — A Kerryman who does volcano impressions.
He fills his navel with talcum powder and coughs.

One Kerryman was showing off his knowledge to another, so he asked him if he knew what shape the world was.
'I don't,' said the second Kerryman. 'Give me a clue.'
'It's the same shape as the buttons on my jacket,' said the first Kerryman.
'Square,' said the second Kerryman.
'That's my Sunday jacket,' said the first Kerryman. 'I meant my weekday jacket. Now what shape is the world?'
'Square on Sundays, round on weekdays,' said the second Kerryman.

Have you heard about the Kerryman who thought that the *Cork Examiner* was a specialist employed in the wine industry?

Have you heard about the Kerryman who took his girlfriend into the Tunnel of Love? They got down to work right away and by the time they came out they had developed three films.

A Corkman who was well known for his anti-apartheid views was buying oranges in a shop owned by a Kerryman. As the Kerryman put the oranges into the bag he was asked if they came from South Africa.
'Yes they do sir,' he told him.
'Put them back,' said the Corkman. 'I won't buy anything that comes from South Africa.'
'I don't blame you sir,' said the Kerryman. 'All those blacks handling them.'

ON A KERRY LORRY

> **NO HAND SIGNALS —**
> **DRIVER EATING HIS YORKIE BAR**

HOW ABOUT

The KERRY FIRING SQUAD that stood around the prisoner in a circle?

The Kerryman who thought an asset was a little donkey?

The Kerryman who was glad he wasn't born in Russia because he didn't speak a word of Russian?

The KERRY MOON ROCKET that didn't quite make it?
It ran out of turf.

The KERRY SHEEPDOG trials where all ten dogs were found guilty?

The Kerryman who always drove with the handbrake on so as to be ready for emergencies?

The Kerryman who liked sandwiches?
When he wasn't very hungry, a pound of butter between two loaves; when he was hungry a bull between two bread vans.

The KERRY SKIER who kept trying to get his ski-pants on over his skis?

The SUPERSTITIOUS KERRY BOXER who attributed his success to the fact that he always carried his lucky horseshoe in his glove?

The GENEROUS KERRY BUSINESSMAN who gave large amounts of money to charity but never signed the cheques because he wanted to remain anonymous?

The Kerryman who thought the Avon Lady was Shakespeare's wife?

The Kerryman who took up yoga to help him quit smoking?
Now he can smoke standing on his head.

The KERRY CAT BURGLAR who stole only cats?

The Kerryman who fooled the income tax people by dropping dead?

The Kerryman who was so ugly a Hallowe'en Mask Company bought up the rights to his face?

The Kerryman who got a job where all he had to do was press a button to start a machine at 8 o'clock and to press it again to stop it at 5 o'clock? He quit because he wanted a less technical job.

The KERRY THRILL-SEEKER who ate his after-eight mints at seven o'clock?

A KERRYMAN'S DESCRIPTION
OF A WELL-KNOWN CORKMAN

I'M NOT SAYING HE'S CRAZY ENOUGH TO BE PUT IN A LOONEY BIN, BUT ON THE OTHER HAND, IF HE WAS IN ONE I DON'T THINK THEY WOULD LET HIM OUT.

PUZZLE CORNER FOR KERRYMEN

1
•

•   •
2   **3**

JOIN THE DOTS TO FORM
A WELL-KNOWN GEOMETRICAL OBJECT

A Kerrywoman was telling a friend that she had over fifty goldfish.
'Where do you keep them?' the friend asked.
'In the bathtub,' she replied.
'But what do you do when you want to take a bath?'
'I blindfold them,' said the Kerrywoman.

A Kerryman went to a riding stable and hired a horse.
'Hold on for a moment,' said the assistant as he helped him on the horse, 'aren't you putting that saddle on backwards.'
'You don't even know which way I want to go.'

Two Kerry farmers met one day at a fair.
'Tell me,' said the first, 'what did you give your mule when he had colic?'
'Turpentine,' said the second.
A few months later they met again.
'What did you say you gave your mule when he had colic?' asked the first.
'Turpentine,' said the second.
'Well I gave my mule turpentine, and he died,' said the first. 'So did mine,' said the second Kerryman, 'so did mine.'

A Kerryman went to England and got the most dangerous job in the country — a lollipop man at Brand's Hatch.

A Kerryman was in the casualty ward of a hospital when he was visited by the Lady Mayoress of the city.
'Now my good man,' she asked him, 'where were you injured?'
'Well mam,' said the Kerryman, 'let me put it this way — if you had been injured where I had been injured, you wouldn't have been injured at all.'

Have you heard about the Kerry swimming Gala that was cancelled because the pool was waterlogged?

A Kerryman called the police to complain about his neighbours. 'Come up here with me and listen to this,' he said to the sergeant, taking him upstairs into the bedroom and beckoning him to put his ear to the wall.
'I can't hear a thing', said the sergeant.
'I know,' said the Kerryman, 'and it's been like that all day.'

How do you recognise a Kerryman in a shoeshop?
He's the one trying on the shoeboxes.

A Kerryman had just been found guilty of a serious crime and the judge asked him if he could pay anything at all towards costs which had also been awarded against him.
'Not a penny your honour,' said the Kerryman. 'Everything I own I've given to my lawyer and three of the jury.'

A Kerryman joined the American Air Force and was making his first parachute jump. The instructor said, 'When you jump out of the plane shout "Geronimo" and pull the rip-cord.'
When the Kerryman woke up in hospital a few days later the first thing he said was, 'What was the name of that Indian again?'

Have you heard about the Kerryman who broke his leg through smoking?
He threw his cigarette end down an   open manhole and tried to step on it.

Two Kerrymen went into a pub, ordered two glasses of water and proceeded to take out their lunch boxes.
'Hold on a minute,' said the barman. 'You're not allowed to eat your own food in here.'
So the two Kerrymen swopped lunch boxes.

Two Kerrymen were in a railway station for the first time and they ran in terror as a train came flying in.
'Do you know what I'm going to tell you,' said one to the other, 'if that thing had come sideways it would have killed the both of us.'

First Kerryman: 'I've just bought one of those new silicon chip hearing aids — it's so small you can hardly see it.'
Second Kerryman: 'That's terrific — does it work well?'
First Kerryman: 'Half past seven.'

Judge: 'The jury have found you guilty.'
Kerryman: 'I know they have but I'm sure your honour has too much intelligence to pay any attention to what that shower of rogues say.'

WHAT TO DO IN KERRY

Go down to the station to watch a train coming in.

Go to see the local barber giving hair-cuts.

Read the tombstones in the cemetery.

See the new bacon slicer in action in the grocery store.

Watch the local alcoholic have delerium tremens.

Watch the lifeguard rescue people from the carwash.

Watch cars being filled with petrol at the filling station.

Call to the local undertakers and ask if he has any empty boxes.

SOMEWHERE IN KERRY

> **PLEASE DO NOT STEAL
> THIS NOTICE**

NEXT DAY IT WAS GONE!